REPAIRING THE DAMAGE

Snow, Ice and Cold

Bernard Stonehouse

NEW DISCOVERY BOOKS

New York

First American publication 1992 by New Discovery Books, Macmillan Publishing Company, 866 Third Avenue, New York, NY 10022

Macmillan Publishing Company is part of the Maxwell Communication Group of Companies.

First published by Evans Brothers Limited, 2A Portman Mansions, Chiltern Street, London W1M 1LE

Printed in Spain by GRAFO, S.A.—Bilbao

10   9   8   7   6   5   4   3   2   1

Stonehouse, Bernard.
        Snow, ice and cold / Bernard Stonehouse.
            p.   cm. — (Repairing the damage)
        Includes index.
        Summary: A look at the damage that snow, ice and cold can cause and at measures that can be taken to minimize the destruction.
        ISBN 0-02-788530-5
        1. Snow—Juvenile literature. 2. Ice—Juvenile literature. 3. Cold—Juvenile literature. [1. Cold. 2. Snow. 3. Ice.] I. Title. II. Series.
        BG2603.8.S76 1992
        910'.911—dc20   92—26298

Acknowledgments

Editor: Su Swallow
Design: Neil Sayer
Production: Jenny Mulvanny

Maps and illustrations: Hardlines, Charlbury

For permission to reproduce copyright material the author and publishers gratefully acknowledge the following:

Cover Robert Harding Picture Library
Title page (Snowblower at work in Churchill, Canada) Norbert Rosing, Bruce Coleman Limited **p4** David Rootes, Poles Apart **p5** B & C Alexander, (inset) John Shaw, Bruce Coleman Limited **p7** Simon Fraser, Science Photo Library **p8** Colin Wyatt, NHPA **p9** (top) Robert Harding Picture Library, (bottom) B & C Alexander **p11** (top left) Peter Johnson, NHPA, (bottom left) British Antarctic Survey, (right) The Hulton Picture Company **p12** A.N.T. (Jonathan Chester), NHPA **p13** B & C Alexander, extract taken from *Icewalk* by Robert Swan, published by Jonathan Cape **p14** B & C Alexander **p15** Keith Gunnar, Bruce Coleman Limited, (inset) Melinda Berge, Bruce Coleman Limited **p16** (top) B & C Alexander, (bottom) The Hulton Picture Company **p17** Norbert Rosing, Bruce Coleman Limited **p18** (top) Doug Allan, Science Photo Library, (middle) Rae/ECOSCENE, (bottom) Steven C. Kaufman, Bruce Coleman Limited **p19** B & C Alexander **p20** Nicholas Devore, Bruce Coleman Limited **p22** Thomas Buchholz, Bruce Coleman Limited **p23** Simon Fraser, Science Photo Library **p24** Robert Harding Picture Library, (inset) Philippa Scott, NHPA **p25** (top left) Stephen Krasemann, NHPA, (top right) B & C Alexander, (bottom) B & C Alexander, NHPA **p26** George Bernard, NHPA, **p27** Bernard Stonehouse **p28** The Hulton Picture Company **p29** Bernard Stonehouse **p30** Robert Harding Picture Library **p31** Sorensen & Olsen, NHPA **p32** Doug Allan, Science Photo Library **p33** Sally Morgan/ECOSCENE, (inset) W Bacon, Science Photo Library **p34** Hawkes/ECOSCENE **p35** Robert Harding Picture Library **p36** Robert Harding Picture Library **p37** Simon Fraser, Science Photo Library **p38** (left) Robert Harding Picture Library, (right) John Cancalosi, Bruce Coleman Limited **p39** Philippa Scott, NHPA **p40** (left) A.N.T. (Jonathan Chester), NHPA, (right) The Hulton Picture Company **p41** B & C Alexander **p42** Bernard Stonehouse **p43** Michael Leach, NHPA

CONTENTS

INTRODUCTION

The past

Humans are not designed for cold climates. With neither fur nor fat in any quantity, we lose heat constantly over our whole body surface. The ancestors of humans were apes, perhaps similar to chimpanzees, who first appeared in the tropics of Africa at a time before the ice age, when all the world was warm. They left the treetops and for millions of years hunted and gathered food on the forest floor and open plains. From the tropics they spread northward into Europe and Asia.

Then came the ice age. Ice caps developed at both ends of the world, first over Antarctica and then, some two to three million years ago, over much of the Arctic. Polar and temperate latitudes became cooler than they had ever been before. Our ancestors were intelligent people, who learned to use fire, to build shelters or live in caves, and to wear the skins of other animals to keep themselves warm. So equipped, they spread far into the north, even living close to the great ice caps that had grown over northern Scandinavia and much of Siberia.

The present

At the start of the 20th century only a few thousand people lived north of the Arctic Circle, and none in the Antarctic. Now even the world's coldest places are inhabited by people. Beyond the Arctic Circle, around the polar ocean, several million brave the long cold winters and short cool summers in villages and towns. Many more live south of the circle in northern Canada and Siberia—areas that in winter are even colder than the Arctic. Most of the settlements have grown from very small beginnings during the past 50 years. Many arose at industrial centers, based on mining for coal, drilling for oil, and similar operations.

The Inuit (Eskimos) and other native peoples of the north have become minorities in their own lands. Today they are heavily outnumbered by newcomers from warmer climates, who work in the Arctic for a few months or years at a time. Natives are well adapted to cold, both mentally and physically. They know how to survive in cold climates, and they pass on their knowledge from generation to generation. Unfortunately, they often lack the skills and knowledge needed for the highly technical jobs that are offered around them. Newcomers to the north may be well equipped for industry, but lack knowledge of how to live in the Arctic, especially how to adapt to the continuous ice and snow, cold and darkness of winter.

Antarctica has no native populations and no industrial developments. Both land and ocean are completely dominated by ice and snow, and Antarctic climates are very much colder than those of the far north. Nobody lives permanently within the Antarctic region. Of the 50 or more small settlements, mostly research stations where scientists and support staff operate, not more than half are occupied all the year round. Fewer than 200 people live at the stations in winter.

Research scientists prepare to dive under pack ice in the Antarctic.

An oil pipeline runs above the frozen ground in Alaska, in the Arctic (main picture). In summer, the snow melts to reveal the tundra vegetation (inset).

Northern Canadian and Siberian town dwellers are likely to see snow and ice on the ground from November to April. In the high Arctic they see them throughout the year. Air temperatures may stay below −4°F for days at a time, and fall overnight to −40°F or lower. Strong winds pack the snow solid and make the cold seem even colder. It seldom rains, but snow may fall several times weekly for months on end. Summer sunshine brings warmth, but in the Arctic tundra this is only enough to thaw a thin top layer of soil. Below that, the ground is permanently frozen solid, up to several miles deep in places. This state of permafrost, as it is called, makes crop-growing and building and pipe-laying very difficult, if not impossible.

There is little agriculture in the Arctic except in coastal Norway. There, warmed by the North Atlantic Drift, sheep and cattle are farmed, and crops are grown well north of the Arctic Circle. Elsewhere it is usually more efficient (though not always cheaper) to ship or fly food in from warmer areas.

Snow and ice produce little direct employment, except as part of the scenic attractions that bring tourists to the Arctic. Many thousands visit each summer, to see snowfields, glaciers, polar wilderness, and wildlife. Tourists need guides, and natives are often the best guides to the Arctic and its animals.

The people who live and work in the Arctic deal with the extremes of a cold climate all year round, using traditional skills as well as modern technology to survive the bitter weather. People who live and work in mountain areas in temperate climates are accustomed to dealing with blizzards, avalanches, and freeze-ups at certain times of year. Yet elsewhere in temperate regions, severe weather continues to cause chaos whenever it arrives. While we cannot alter the world weather patterns dramatically, there are many ways of improving our efficiency in preventing damage caused by snow, ice, and cold and learning the many basic survival skills that are essential for anyone whose work or leisure takes them to cold places.

CHAPTER ONE

ARCTIC ADVENTURE

Early pioneers

Some 20,000 to 30,000 years ago small bands of hunters spread into northeastern Siberia. They were slightly built people, probably standing about 4 feet tall, and looking much like smaller versions of modern man. They dressed in skins and carried tools of bone, stone, and wood. Some crossed eastward into North America over what is now the Bering Strait. At the time it was dry land, for this was a cold spell of the ice age, when huge sheets of ice covered the far north, and sea level the world over was over 300 feet lower than at present.

Many of these hardy people spread southward into the warmer forests, where they became the ancestors of the Indians of North and South America. Others remained in the north, keeping to the coasts and rivers. From them, perhaps from further waves of Siberian hunters, came the northern people that today we call Inuit (the name by which most Eskimos prefer to be called). We know little of these true pioneers of Arctic life, for they left very little record of any kind.

The first Europeans to explore the Arctic fringes were a few dozen Christian monks from Britain and Norway. They braved the ocean in tiny sailing craft no bigger than modern rowboats. Their journeys were made in the fifth and sixth centuries, 500 years before the Vikings and 1,000 years before the merchant adventurers.

Blown westward and north into the region of snow and ice, these voyagers were probably the first men to visit and live on parts of Greenland, Iceland, and Svalbard. They were almost certainly the first to see frozen sea, and experience the ice, snow, and cold of the Arctic at firsthand. From their travels they brought back fabulous stories of whales, walruses, and snow-white bears, and accounts of miraculous crystal pillars in marble seas—the first known descriptions of icebergs in pack ice.

Greenland saga

On a summer day just over 1,000 years ago a band of Viking sailors set sail from Iceland in search of a new home. Eventually they reached the rocky shore of a windswept country which their leader, Erik the Red, had discovered during a previous voyage and had called Greenland. There was ice in the sea, and snow and ice high on the mountains behind the coast, but to the Vikings, it seemed no worse than the Icelandic shores they had left behind, and as good a place as any to settle.

Soon the first cottages were being built; turf, brushwood, and rocks from the shore were the building materials. The ships returned to Iceland to spread the good news and bring out more families. Winter brought heavy snowfalls and strong winds. In the fjords the sea filled with slush, and ice crackled in the fishing nets. Already used to hard living, the new Greenlanders made themselves sheepskin clothing, found enough timber to keep their fires going, and sat out the winter in comfort. In spring they greeted a new batch of Viking immigrants. Before long they had formed two communities, each of several hundred men, women, and children, on the coast of southwestern Greenland.

Ships plied frequently between these settlements, linking them with Iceland and Norway. The settlers traded surplus wool and fish for lumber, iron, and other goods that they could not find locally. They built stone houses and churches. The villages became permanent settlements, and the communities flourished for three centuries or more.

An early account of the Greenland settlements appears in *The King's Mirror*, a 13th-century Norwegian manuscript. We do not know who the writer was, but he seems to have talked to travelers who had returned from Greenland, and tried to write truthfully:

A fjord of southern Greenland in summer, which must have looked much the same when the Viking settlers landed.

"Nobody knows whether the land is large or small, because all the mountain ranges and all the valleys are covered with ice, and no opening has been found anywhere. Men have often tried to go up into the country and climb the highest mountains in various places to look about and learn whether any land could be found that was free from ice and habitable. But nowhere have they found such a place, except what is now occupied, which is a little strip along the water's edge. . . . The great majority in that country do not know what bread is, never having seen it. But men can live on food other than bread. It is reported that the pasturage is good and that there are large and fine farms in Greenland. The farmers raise cattle and sheep in large numbers and make butter and cheese in great quantities. The people subsist chiefly on these foods, and on beef; but they also eat the flesh of various kinds of game, such as reindeer, whales, seals, and bears."

Climate change

After 200 years of settlement, things began to go wrong. We do not know the full story, for the settlers left few written records. Most of what we know of them and their sad history has been found by digging in the sites. The main cause of their decline in fortune seems to have been a change in climate, a cooling that spread snow, ice, and chill all over Europe during the early Middles Ages. Forest timber, the main household fuel, became scarce and expensive, and the poorer people suffered greatly from cold. In the far north the Greenland Vikings were among the first to feel the changes, and to suffer severely from its consequences.

Winters grew harsher, with the ground frozen and winter snows staying longer on the pastures. Summers shortened and became cooler, leaving little time for fruit and grain to ripen. The fjords and bays of southern Greenland were choked with sea ice from early winter to late summer. Fishing became difficult; trading ships from Norway and Iceland were lost at sea, foundering among fog, snow, and ice. Eventually the risks were too great; few fishermen ventured out and the traders ceased to call, leaving the communities isolated.

Buildings fell into disrepair, and ill health struck the Greenlanders. Skeletons of men, women, and children dug from graves in the settlements show that many suffered malnutrition and died young, long before their time. We do not know when the last survivors died. Some were still there in the early 16th century, but Martin Frobisher, an explorer who visited later in 1578, reported the villages deserted, the farms empty, and the churches in ruins. Snow, ice, and cold had descended, and the south Greenland settlements had gone.

Since then the Arctic fringe has warmed slightly, and farmers and fishermen live once again in the fjords of southern Greenland. Could the cold return? Yes, almost certainly, and it could spread much farther into the temperate regions of the northern hemisphere, just as it did during the coldest periods of the ice age. But this will not happen soon or quickly; when it does, some thousands of years from now, we shall have plenty of warning, and be much better able to deal with it than were the Greenlanders of long ago.

The Inuit example

Where the Vikings failed, the Inuit succeeded. Inuit ways of life, developed over many centuries, lasted almost to the present day. Most modern Inuit now live settled lives similar to our own, but the old ways can still be seen in some of their communities. They lived in small family groups that were constantly on the move, traveling with the seasons in search of food. They spent the short summers hunting and trapping on the tundra, taking foxes, reindeer, and other animals for meat and skins, catching fish from the rivers and fish, seals, and whales along the coast. During the much longer winters they lived at the coast or out on the sea

A fishing community in west Greenland, where in winter the sea is frozen over and fishing boats are held fast in the ice.

This man has caught several halibut through a hole in the winter sea ice, off the east coast of Greenland.

ice, where they could fish and catch seals through holes in the ice.

Summer houses were built of turf, stones, skins, and driftwood. In winter they made houses from blocks of ice and tightly packed snow, which were much warmer and more comfortable than they sound. The Inuit lived simply, traveling with all their possessions in boats made from sealskins or on sledges made from driftwood and bones.

Each group learned how to survive in the area in which it lived. They had no written language until the end of the 19th century, so the skills of hunting and gathering food were taught by parents to their children. How to cut and stitch skins to make clothing, where to spend each season, and how to survive when conditions were bad—all this was passed in songs and stories from generation to generation.

During medieval times some of the Inuit people of western Greenland, traveling southward down the coast, by chance met the Vikings of the northern Greenland settlement, which was already in decline. This was one of the earliest meetings of Inuit and Europeans. Unfor-

An Inuit hunter builds an igloo.

tunately, we know nothing of what they said to each other or thought of each others' ways. Perhaps the settlers learned some useful tricks of hunting and survival from the Inuit. More probably they regarded them as savages, uncouth and ungodly; that was unfortunately how most Europeans regarded Arctic natives, with no regard for their many skills of survival. Yet there is no doubt as to which was the better equipped when snow, ice, and cold took charge along the Greenland coast. It was the Inuit, not the settlers, who survived.

CHAPTER TWO

POLAR CHALLENGE

The north polar region (Arctic) is a sea basin almost surrounded by land. If you stand at the North Pole, you are on an ice floe 6 to 10 feet thick, with a deep ocean beneath your feet. There is nothing to see but other ice floes, and the nearest point of land is northern Greenland, over 400 miles away. The south polar region (Antarctic) is a huge continent, larger than Australia or the United States, almost completely covered with permanent ice. Standing at the South Pole, you are in the middle of a huge ice plain almost two miles thick.

There is no human settlement at the North Pole, because the sea ice is too thin for safety, and drifting all the time. At the South Pole there is a permanently manned U.S. scientific station, partly buried in snow.

During the past century, men from all over the world have accepted the challenge to explore these inhospitable regions. Some have succeeded, others have failed. The stories of their experiences vividly portray the problems of snow, ice, and cold and how they can be overcome.

Death in Antarctica

One day in March 1912, in a small tent on the Ross Ice Shelf, Antarctica, the last survivor of five brave explorers penciled a few final, shaky words in his diary. "We shall stick it out to the end," he wrote, "but we are getting weaker of course and the end cannot be far. It seems a pity but I do not think I can write more."

The writer was Captain Robert Scott of the Royal Navy, age 43 and well known throughout the world as an experienced polar explorer.

The five who died were members of the British National Antarctic Expedition. They had set out from their base camp in November 1911, attempting to be the first to reach the South Pole. When they arrived at the pole, on January 18, they made a shattering discovery. A five-man party from a rival Norwegian expedition had arrived on December 16, just over one month earlier. Traveling by a different route and using dog teams, the Norwegians under Roald Amundsen had beaten them to the pole and

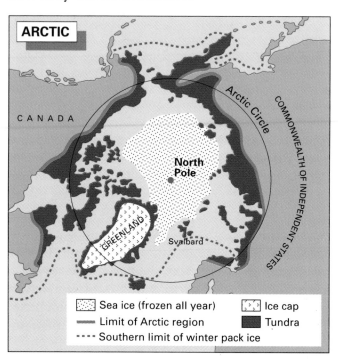

ARCTIC

CANADA

Arctic Circle

COMMONWEALTH OF INDEPENDENT STATES

North Pole

GREENLAND

Svalbard

Sea ice (frozen all year)   Ice cap
Limit of Arctic region   Tundra
Southern limit of winter pack ice

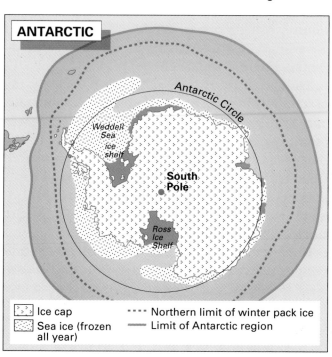

ANTARCTIC

Antarctic Circle

Weddell Sea ice shelf

South Pole

Ross Ice Shelf

Ice cap   Northern limit of winter pack ice
Sea ice (frozen all year)   Limit of Antarctic region

Captain Scott (right) and his team climbed the Beardmore Glacier (above) on their way to the South Pole, but they failed to return to the main base camp (top, Scott's hut).

departed, leaving a tent, a note, and a criss-crossing pattern of tracks in the snow to mark their passage.

Saddened and downhearted, the British party turned homeward. It was now late in the season, and the five exhausted men found themselves enduring harsh conditions of snow, ice, and extreme cold. On the return journey down the Beardmore Glacier one suffered serious frost-bite, blistered feet, and a fall that left him shaken and perhaps internally injured. He became delirious, and was the first to die. A second, badly crippled by frostbite and knowing that he would never complete the long haul back to base, walked away from the tent to die alone. Scott and his two remaining companions continued as long as they could before setting up their final camp.

Why did they die?

Explorers and others have argued for years over reasons for the Scott disaster. There was faulty planning, the rations were inadequate, the work of hauling heavy sledges by hand was almost unendurably hard. The route to the South Pole crosses a region where snow, ice, and cold reign supreme. Nowhere else in the world are conditions quite so tough and hostile for human beings; nowhere is there less room for mistakes in planning.

It is tempting to think that Scott and his companions died of cold, but this is an oversimplification. The cold encountered by the explorers was no worse than that experienced during cold spells every winter by people living in

In some ways, polar equipment has changed little since Scott's day, but the materials used are much lighter.

northern Canada, Alaska, and Siberia. Cold was, however, an important component of the disaster. The clothing and equipment of the polar party, though the best available at the time, was far from adequate by modern standards. After months in the field their reindeer-skin sleeping bags were permanently wet from condensation. Woolen inner and outer clothing would have lost much of their insulating properties. Most important of all, their windproof coveralls, torn and dirty from months of hard wear, no longer kept out the chilling wind.

When the tent with the bodies of Scott and his men was found by a search party a few months later, it lay almost buried under accumulating snow. The bodies were frozen, but in the center of the tent stood two items that, in part at least, explained their deaths. One was a ration box with very little food remaining; the other was a paraffin stove that had run out of fuel.

The main cause of their deaths was almost certainly malnutrition—a combination of inadequate diet and starvation over a period of weeks —rather than cold. Traveling had proved slower and more difficult than they had planned for. There were many days with weather so bad that they could not travel at all, though they still had to eat. Eventually their carefully rationed stocks of food and fuel ran out. Sad to say, it happened within a few miles of their next depot, where plenty of both were waiting.

The shortage of paraffin for the stove was due to leaking containers, which may have been caused, as Scott himself assumed, by careless sealing when they were filled. However, scientists now suspect that cold, rather than carelessness, caused the leaks. In extreme cold lead tends to crumble from a solid to a powdery form. The cold of the plateau depots may have weakened the lead solder that held the cans together, making it porous and allowing the contents to leak away into the snow.

Whatever the cause, shortage of fuel meant that the travelers could not warm themselves or dry their clothes. Warming is not usually critical for healthy people who can keep themselves warm with exercise, though it would have been a great comfort for Scott and his companions during their final, immobile days. Drying out clothing is a more serious matter, for icy or damp clothing draws heat from the body—heat that cannot be afforded by hungry men when air temperatures are well below zero.

Cold affected the party in other ways, even to the snow they were traveling over. Snow that is close to freezing point melts slightly when sledge runners slide over it. By contrast, in

Sastrugi—ridges in the snow carved by the wind—add to the problems of sledding in the polar regions.

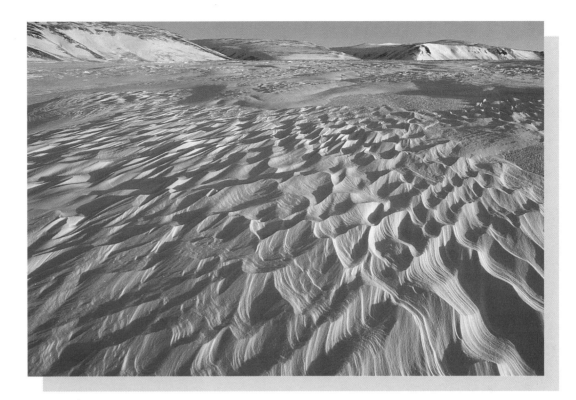

temperatures of −4°F to −22°F cold, wind-blown snow provides a rough, sandy surface that makes sledding particularly difficult. "The surface layer," Scott wrote in his diary, "... is coated with a thin layer of woolly crystals" that "... cause impossible friction on the runners." Cold snow becomes very hard, almost as abrasive as sand, and tough enough to erode rocks. During the blizzards that the polar party encountered almost every day, this hard snow blasted constantly into their faces and clothing.

In a warmer climate the explorers would certainly have survived longer. In Antarctic cold, without a daily intake of high-calorie food, they could not maintain their body temperatures. However, there were other and probably more important dietary problems. In the early 20th century little was known of vitamins and essential minerals. Apart from a simple shortage of food, their sledding ration lacked much in the way of nutrients that would today be included without question. After five months of back-breaking work on inadequate rations, the men had almost certainly used up their own bodies' reserves of fat, protein, vitamins, and essential minerals. They were probably suffering from scurvy, due to lack of vitamin C, and a long-term malfunctioning of muscles and nerves that they would have summed up as "exhaustion"—due mainly to the other deficiencies in their diet.

The windchill factor

In 1989 a group of eight men from seven countries walked to the North Pole. It took them 56 days. They had the benefit of carefully balanced diets, modern equipment, and radio communications, but these advantages were still no match against the fierce cold. The leader of the expedition, Robert Swan, described the effects of the cold in his book *Icewalk*:

"After the fire was extinguished, we had the usual revolting breakfast of muesli, pemmican and hot chocolate and were on our way. A small wind had sprung up, giving a venomous sting to the cold. Exposure to Arctic cold for a few seconds in calm conditions will do no more than give you pins and needles. Let there be just a hint of a breath of wind, however, and you are in for an experience to remember. The wind sucks heat from your body by constantly changing the air around it, greatly increasing the feeling of cold. Icy winds can transform a moderately cold temperature into one of bitter intensity. This is known as the windchill factor. You're not in the Arctic long before you know a lot about it. . . . Some of us wore huge fox hats given us by Misha. Fur and animal skin were the best defense against extreme cold. Earlier explorers had paid little heed to the Inuit's caribou skin pants and jackets, seal skin boots and fur hoods, and suffered the consequences. . . . All the same, no matter how well prepared you are, there is nothing that is a match for the Arctic cold in the morning. The mucus in my nose froze. If the wind was up the water in my eyes also froze. Vaporous breath was caught in beards or on chins and formed huge unsightly lumps. . . . Plastic shrank and all foods and liquids were frozen solid. Hot drinks began to freeze while you were consuming them. Pen ink became a solid mass, batteries died and it would take more than five minutes to light a candle because the wax was too cold to melt. If you exposed your fingers to the air they would be frozen in five seconds.

The only way to keep the intense cold at bay was to march all day."

Blowing cold

Windchill is the chilling effect of wind on air temperature. There are several ways of calculating windchill. The most effective ways take into account your skin temperature and the amount of clothing you are likely to be wearing. In a typical example, 14°F in calm air, 50°F in a wind of 5 knots, and 59°F at 10 knots all give the same windchill of 500. Similarly, a windchill of 1,000 is experienced at −58°F with no wind, at 19.4°F in a light wind, and at 32°F in a strong wind.

Recipe for survival

We know now that the best recipe for survival in a cold climate is to be well fed, well clothed, and healthy, with good circulation and body reserves. Activity is generally the best way of keeping warm, for heat generated by muscular action spreads quickly throughout the body. If fingers, face, and toes are warm, the whole body feels comfortable.

A Canadian Inuit wears furs to protect him against temperatures of down to −49°F.

In a real emergency, the will to survive is all-important. Cold saps energy, and fear and a sense of helplessness often quickly follow. Keeping active is usually good for morale, though moving on is not always wise. Lost in a dangerous place in bad visibility, it may well be safer to camp where you are than to travel into the unknown. It makes good sense to prepare the best possible camp while the energy lasts (see page 15). Hunger causes anxiety, so emergency rations are essential, preferably ready-prepared foods that are easily digested and rich in energy-giving sugars and fats.

Where activity is impossible, good insulation becomes important. This includes warm dry clothing, quilts, sleeping bags, and means of keeping the wind off. Traveling parties need always to plan for the possibility of one member becoming immobilized, perhaps through injury. An injured person needs extra protection from cold, and the quickest possible transfer to safety and warmth.

Modern lightweight tents (main picture) collapse very small, and provide excellent shelter against cold winds and extreme temperatures. If no tent is available, a snow cave (inset) is better than an igloo, if the snow is deep enough.

Building a snow shelter

In bad weather with cold winds and blowing snow, almost any shelter is better than none. It is not difficult to make a snow shelter, as long as the snow is dry and deep, and there is plenty of it. If you are caught out in bad weather and cannot get home, a simple shelter may keep you warm for a few critical hours, and help to save your life.

Best for protecting you is hard, wind-packed snow—the kind that forms drifts on the sheltered side of walls and buildings. If you can find a big enough drift, dig your way into it, and hollow it out to make a cave. Keep the entrance as small as you can, and close it with snow blocks once you are inside. Make the cave big enough to give you plenty of air. Once you are out of the wind, your own body heat will keep the space surprisingly warm. Two or three people in a snow cave help to keep each other warm.

It is important to stay as dry as you can: Brush the snow from your clothing before it melts, and lie on groundsheets or waterproof plastic if possible.

On tundra or open fields where there are no natural windbreaks, build a wall of snow blocks, and sit or lie in its shelter, keeping the snow off you with anything waterproof. If the snow is firm and deep enough, you may be able to build a snow house. Mark out a circle seven to ten feet in diameter. Use a spade or knife to cut blocks of snow from within the circle, and build them into a wall around the circumference. Use the biggest blocks you can manage, so that you build quickly. When you have used up all the snow inside, take more blocks from outside. Shape the blocks to fit closely together. The Inuit trim them so that they spiral inward to form a dome (see page 9). This takes practice; in an emergency you may have to be content with spreading a groundsheet over the top, holding it in place with more blocks.

CHAPTER THREE

TRAVEL PROSPECTS

On foot

After Scott's time very few explorers tried to walk long distances over snow and ice. Even in his day there were more efficient methods of polar travel; today there are more again, brought about by the invention of over-snow vehicles and aircraft. Hauling by hand is still done for recreation and to show it is possible; parties have recently skied or marched to both poles, mainly for the challenge (see page 13). Those who travel by more modern methods—snowmobile, tractor, or aircraft, for example—need to know something of the old techniques, for they risk the possibility of mechanical breakdown. It pays them to know how to survive until they are rescued, or can find their

Snow shoes are useful in soft snow among trees, where long skis would be impractical.

Captain Scott and others hauling a sledge over the ice in the Antarctic.

own way to safety.

Hauling by hand is hard work and hopelessly inefficient. People in harness are the wrong shape for dragging heavy loads efficiently; at best they can pull little more than 55 pounds each, making 25 miles per day. Scott's Manchurian ponies did better. They could pull over 550 pounds each on firm surfaces, though they floundered hopelessly in soft snow. Their main drawback was the huge bulk of fodder—oats and bran mash—required to keep them working properly in the very low temperatures.

Sled dogs are far more efficient for polar work. As Amundsen knew very well, a team of nine huskies can pull a sledge with a total load of over 1,450 pounds on good surfaces, rather less through soft snow. Their food, whether frozen seal meat or specially prepared pemmican, is more compact than oats and bran mash, and needs less preparation.

Engine power

Ernest Shackleton pioneered the use of motor vehicles in Antarctica, in 1907. His Arrol-Johnston roadster proved difficult to start in low temperatures. Once started, it traveled successfully over hard sea ice but quickly bogged down in snow. Scott experimented seriously with gasoline driven tractors. His primitive tractor cars, fitted with chainlike caterpillar treads, traveled well at first, but broke down on the polar journey within a few miles of starting out, and had to be abandoned. However, Scott had high hopes for the future success of tractors. In his diary he wrote of "their ability to revolutionize polar transportation," and events proved him right. Today, tracked motor vehicles of all kinds have become the normal means of surface travel over snow and ice.

Caterpillar tracks driven by pinion wheels distribute the weight of a vehicle over a much larger area than tires, preventing both slipping and sinking into the snow. In 1930, the American explorer Richard Evelyn Byrd experimented with Citroën automobiles on which tracks replaced the rear wheels. They worked in different kinds of snow, but both engines and tracks proved unreliable. Byrd continued to use dog teams, backed by aircraft, for his main overland journeys.

After World War II, several kinds of surplus tracked vehicles were taken to Antarctica, and new ones were invented to use in both polar regions. However, among the cheapest and most successful have been standard agricultural tractors with continuous tracks, used over many

Dogs pulling a dogsled in Canada.

Transportation at the poles: (above) A Sno-cat tows a sledge of clean snow for drinking water, (left) snow vehicles take tourists across Arctic snowfields, and (below) a "train" includes laboratories and accommodation for an oil survey team.

kinds of icy surface. Three Ferguson tractors of the Commonwealth Trans-Antarctic Expedition, hauling "cabooses" or plywood cabins on sledges, reached the South Pole on January 3, 1958, after a grueling journey over rough sastrugi (see photograph on page 13). They were driven from McMurdo Sound by Sir Edmund Hillary and his New Zealand colleagues, and were the first motor vehicles ever to reach the South Pole overland.

Shortly afterward, on January 19, they were joined by a group of more complex, specially constructed snow tractors called Sno-cats, which British explorers led by Dr. Vivian Fuchs had driven from the opposite side of Antarctica. Sno-cats are made up of a cabin on a chassis, with four separate tracks.

American and Russian explorers use trains of massive tracked vehicles specially designed for transportation over snow. Each vehicle is as big as a long-distance coach with sleeping quarters and mess rooms. Each carries several tons of equipment on board. In Antarctica they are used for long-distance journeys: Russian scientists use them to replenish their high-plateau scientific stations. These huge vehicles are warm, but they are noisy and uncomfortable, rocking and rolling over the rough surfaces enough to make their passengers seasick.

On a much smaller scale, snowmobiles have become the standard personal vehicle, largely replacing dog teams. Like a motorcycle on skis, with a small gasoline engine and caterpillar track for propulsion, a snowmobile travels faster than walking pace over rough snow, carrying a driver and passenger and hauling a loaded sledge.

In the air

The first flights in Antarctica were made in two balloons, flown by explorers in 1902 for reconnaissance over the sea ice. The first Antarctic fixed-wing flights were made in 1928 and 1929, in a Lockheed Vega monoplane. The pilot was Australian explorer Sir Hubert Wilkins, who took photographs over the Antarctic Peninsula. Richard Byrd used aircraft in all his expeditions from 1929 onward. Helicopters were flown widely by United States naval expeditions after World War II, proving their worth in reconnaissance flights over sea ice, and landing stores

An Inuit hunter drives a snowmobile.

A light aircraft fitted with skis lands to check that all is well with two Canadian trappers.

and parties of surveyors in remote places. Large fixed-wing aircraft, taking off and landing on skis, were used by several nations during the International Geophysical Year expeditions of 1957–1959, making widespread photographic and scientific flights over many areas of the continent never before seen by humans.

Today both fixed-wing aircraft and helicopters are widely employed for exploration. The South Pole itself, once the world's loneliest, remotest point, now has a permanent station occupied year-round by scientists and technicians, both men and women. During the summer, aircraft fly in almost every day with supplies, equipment, and visitors. The journey from McMurdo Sound to the South Pole, which took Scott two and a half months on foot and Hillary over a month by tractor, takes less than a morning by a four-engined aircraft, in far greater safety and comfort than Scott could have dreamed possible.

But flying in the Antarctic is not without its problems. One morning a few years ago a small, single-engined light aircraft set off from a research station in Antarctica to carry supplies over a ridge of mountains and land them at a depot site. On board were a pilot and copilot, and a surveyor whose job it would be to "fix" the site of the depot. The aircraft took off on skis and headed across the mountains. Just over an hour later it landed safely in soft snow almost at sea level. The pilots unloaded the supplies (in-tended for use by a sledding party later in the year), while the surveyor set up a theodolite and measured the angles of distant mountain peaks. This took about two hours. Then the little aircraft took off for the return flight. One pilot recalls:

"Now troubles began. Thick clouds appeared and began to roll over the mountain peaks. Ice formed on the wings, so that the aircraft was slowed down, and unable to climb to full height. Snow filled the air, streaming off the cabin windows and making it almost impossible to see anything. We knew of a glacier-filled valley just off our course, that would allow us to cross the mountains at less than 1300 meters (4,270 feet). We headed for it, only dimly seeing the mountains on either side, and the glacier below that rose suddenly to meet us.

"Slowed by the winds, it took us over an hour to reach the highest point of the valley floor: then, after crossing a ridge, we were heading down another glacier that would return us to sea level on the homeward side of the mountains.

"Still barely able to see, we skimmed down the valley only a few feet above the glacier surface, twisting and turning to avoid jagged rock faces that loomed toward us out of the snowstorm. Now the engine began to cough and splutter; ice was filling the air intake and causing loss of power. Just a few kilometers further on, half gliding, half flying, we saw the ice cliff marking the end of the glacier passing beneath us. Now we were back over sea ice, and knew it was safe to land.

"Or so it should have been—but luck was no longer with us. With just a few meters to spare we turned into wind and touched down on what looked like a patch of smooth, firm snow. But the sea ice beneath the snow was rough, with hidden blocks of hard ice beneath a thin snow cover. As the skis sank into the snow, one hit a lump of ice and shattered against it. The aircraft spun, tipped up on its nose and turned over, coming to rest in a shattered heap.

"Fortunately we were unharmed, though the radio was useless and we could not tell our base where we were. Still over 150 km (100 miles) from home, we began the long march over the sea ice that eventually brought us back to safety."

How do aircraft pilots cope with ice and snow? They have to be weather-wise and know how to cope with the dangers that come up from time to time. Most of the hazards occur on the ground or in a bad weather zone within a few hundred yards above the ground. Jet aircraft of commercial airlines, flying at 33,000 to 43,000 feet, are high above the bad weather systems. The air they fly through is very cold—it might be −40°F or lower—but there is little moisture at that height and very little risk of icing (ice forming on wings and propellers).

Taking off in cold weather and in snowstorms can be especially dangerous. Snow makes it difficult to see ahead, and a pilot may lose his sense of direction and balance. Navigational instruments, usually very reliable, may be put out of action by ice. The greatest danger is from ice forming on wings and propellers. This happens when a cold aircraft flies through near-freezing rain, which splashes onto the surfaces and freezes into a solid sheet. Ice building up rapidly can alter the shape of the wings and reduce their ability to hold the aircraft up in the air. It can quite suddenly add a lot of weight, making it difficult for the aircraft to climb or even to stay in the air. In gasoline engines ice can form in the carburetor air intake, choking it and preventing air from getting into the engine.

Landing in ice and snow can be difficult: It is often hard for a pilot to judge his height above a clean snow surface. In fog and snowstorms, snow and sky blend into "whiteout" conditions that are especially dangerous. Helicopters hovering over soft snow raise a cloud of snow that obscures the pilot's vision, until the down-draft has swept all the loose snow away.

Hot air is used to de-ice and protect the wings and tailplane.

Hot air, and heat from the engine oil supply, protect the engine.

Keeping aircraft ice-free

Like all modern passenger and freight aircraft, the BA 146 is designed to prevent the buildup of ice. It uses hot air from each of its four engines to prevent the aircraft from icing up. The hot air is piped along fine tubes to the leading edges of the wings and tailplane, and to three main parts of the engines themselves. Once the hot air has circulated, it escapes from vents on the aircraft body. The aircraft is also fitted on the outside with an ice detector, linked to a warning signal on the flight deck, and floodlights on the wings allow checks to be made at night.

CHAPTER FOUR

ICE AT SEA

End of a cruise

On a fine evening in June 1989 the Russian cruise liner *Maxim Gorky* plowed northward across the Norwegian Sea, en route from Iceland to Svalbard. The liner carried a crew of 378 and 575 passengers, tourists enjoying a summer cruise that would take them to the Arctic. The sea was calm, with a long swell that hardly troubled the liner. At 18.5 knots, almost top speed, they were making good progress. The captain expected to meet ice somewhere along the route, for Svalbard lies well north of the Arctic Circle, and even in summer is often surrounded by pack ice. Before him on the bridge was a chart, received by radio some hours before, showing that the ice edge lay just a mile or so ahead. Two officers were keeping a close lookout for it, and so was the ship's radar, for sea ice can damage a ship, even a modern ship built of strong sheet steel. Though it was late evening, the sun was still above the horizon, and the light still good enough to see well ahead.

Then quite suddenly they entered a belt of fog—cold, damp air that meant the pack ice was very close. Before they had time to slow down, heavy floes of ice up to 16 feet thick seemed to surround the ship. They swung to port, but the starboard bow hit one of the floes with an impact that was felt by everyone on board. In seconds the steel bow plates were holed in three places along the waterline. The sea poured in, and the ship began listing to starboard. The passengers and crew were ordered overboard into lifeboats and rafts. The swell, hardly noticeable aboard the ship, suddenly became important. The ice, now surrounding the ship, was heaving up and down, grinding the lifeboats against the ship's side and trapping them between the floes. It proved safer to land the passengers onto the ice itself to await

The Russian cruiser *Maxim Gorky*, in a fjord in Norway.

Ice floes off Svalbard. Those that damaged the *Maxim Gorky* were perhaps five times as thick.

rescue, by helicopters and ships, which arrived in response to radio messages. Everyone was taken off the ice within a few hours.

It seems almost incredible that ice can damage a modern ship with thick steel plates. However, the *Maxim Gorky* was only one of the latest of many ships to be damaged or sunk by ice. Curiously, older wooden ships often fare better than modern steel ships, for they travel more slowly and their hulls are more flexible and resistant to impact.

The largest and most powerful modern icebreakers are built of steel, reinforced internally and with plates especially hardened and thickened at the waterline. Yet even these are at risk if they try to enter really heavy Arctic or Antarctic pack ice.

How the sea freezes

The pack ice floes that cover polar oceans begin as tiny ice crystals, which form when surface waters chill to freezing point. As the sea water is salty, the ice forms not at 32°F (the freezing point of fresh water) but at a slightly lower temperature of 28.76°F. The freezing process separates the water from its dissolved salts, so the crystals that form are salt-free. On cold, clear autumn nights, when the air is well below freezing point and the sea loses its surface heat rapidly, the crystals form quickly over areas of thousands of square feet, making a thick, gray, porridgelike layer at the surface.

After one or two days of intense cold, the

"porridge" has hardened into a crust of ice, perhaps 4 to 8 inches thick. There is usually enough wave movement at the sea surface to break the crust into "pancakes"—round plates of ice about a foot and a half across, often with edges thickened from rubbing together. Further chilling causes the water between the pancakes to freeze, so the resulting ice has a mottled appearance.

As winter wears on, the ice thickens by additions from below. Heavy snowfall settles on its surface, weighing it down so that seawater floods over it, freezes, and adds even more to its thickness. By the end of winter most sea ice, by then a few months old, is thick and firm enough even for light aircraft to land on skis. "Fast ice" of this kind (so called because it is fast, or close, to the coast) is seldom quite smooth. Tidal movements and winds blowing across it cause tensions that break it up into floes with "leads" of open water between.

Much of the ice breaks away from the land in summer and drifts off toward the open sea, becoming what seamen have long called pack ice—floes of various sizes and thicknesses, often forming "fields" hundreds of miles across, that drift with winds and currents. Much of the pack ice eventually drifts into warmer seas, where it melts and disappears. Some, however, like that in the Arctic Ocean basin and parts of Antarctica, drifts into cold backwater areas and fails to melt. Next winter it thickens further, mostly by additions of snow.

Multiyear ice may persist for decades, growing slowly in thickness all the time. In Antarctica the Weddell Sea has a core of such ice, several yards thick and almost impenetrable by ships. The Arctic Ocean, too, has a central mass of floes that circulate for many years, eventually escaping to drift southward in a current that flows along the eastern flank of Greenland. The ice floes 16 feet thick that the *Maxim Gorky* encountered were almost certainly from this source.

Ice in Antarctica: (inset) pancake ice and (main picture) gulls on pack ice

Leads between floes (left) are a blessing for whales and seals, which need open water for surfacing to breathe. Polar bears (above, on new ice) swim across leads to hunt for seals resting on the ice.

Wildlife at the surface

Sea ice less than a year old is almost transparent, letting light through to its undersurface and providing a spring breeding ground for marine algae, the microscopic plants of surface waters. Shrimp and other tiny crustaceans crawl about the undersurface of the floes, browsing on the algae. They in turn become the food of fish and seabirds.

Seals climb out onto the floes to rest in the sun, and several species give birth to their pups and raise them on the sea ice far from land. Polar bears swim across leads to hunt for seals on the inshore fast ice; walruses, which feed on the seabed in shallow water, come up to rest on the ice floes and warm themselves in the sun. Birds, too, use the floes for resting, and the open water between them is their feeding area. Some species of polar birds, for example snow petrels, feed only among the pack ice; it is rare to see them anywhere else except on their breeding cliffs ashore. Antarctic penguins of several species ride the ice floes. One species, the black

and white Adélie penguin, nests on the Antarctic coast but moves out onto the pack ice in winter, because then the sea is warmer than the land. Another species, the colorful emperor penguin, incubates eggs and raises chicks on the winter sea ice, breeding through the coldest period so that its chicks can be ready for independence by the summer.

Harp seals in a lead of open water off the coast of Canada.

Whalers and explorers

The pack ice forms a barrier to polar lands, complete in winter and patchy in summer, and always dangerous for expedition ships. The early explorers from temperate lands marveled at these huge expanses of frozen sea. Throughout the 17th, 18th and early 19th centuries they sailed northward year after year from Britain and Europe, hoping to discover a northeast passage across the top of Asia, or a northwest passage across the top of North America, that would lead them to the riches of China and the East Indies.

Their tiny wooden sailing ships, most of them no bigger than modern fishing boats, returned summer after summer to enter the pack ice and force their way through as far as they could. Some discovered the breeding grounds of walruses, which the explorers killed for their valuable ivory tusks. Some found great concentrations of whales, starting an Arctic whaling industry that lasted for two centuries or more.

Experienced captains learned the annual movements of the ice. After tossing on rough oceans for weeks beforehand, entering the edge of the pack ice was always something of a relief for the crew of a small ship. They looked for leads between the floes that would take them in the right direction, often to the open water and the whaling grounds that they knew lay beyond.

However, a sudden change of wind could bring many tons of ice bearing down on the ships. Occasionally whole fleets of whaling ships were caught in this way and crushed, leaving

An 18th century Dutch whaling fleet in the Arctic.

their crews stranded on the pack ice.

Explorers took even greater risks. Often less experienced and less cautious than whalers, they pressed forward into the unknown and frequently got themselves into difficulties from which there was no escape. The U.S. naval vessel *Jeanette*, for example, trying to reach the North Pole through the Bering Strait in 1879, was caught by the ice and carried for almost two years along the Siberian coast. She was finally crushed and sunk off the New Siberian Islands; only a few of her crew survived.

By a curious chance, spars and other wreckage discovered three years later among pack ice off southwest Greenland were identified as belonging to the *Jeanette*. This showed clearly that strong currents were carrying the Arctic pack ice across the polar ocean. The discovery prompted Fridtjof Nansen, the Norwegian explorer, to design and build *Fram*, a ship with a rounded bottom, that would rise out of the pack ice under pressure. *Fram* sailed north in 1893 into the Laptev Sea, close to the Lena River delta, and in a three-year journey drifted safely with the ice across the Arctic basin to Svalbard.

Icebreakers

Almost every Arctic country has one or more icebreaking ships in its national fleet. The Commonwealth of Independent States, with its immense length of Arctic coastline, operates about 20 large icebreakers each summer, keeping open the Northern Sea Route for several months (usually from April to November) so that the northern ports can operate. The largest icebreakers maintain the oceanic supply lanes, escorting passenger and cargo ships, and rescuing any that get into difficulties with ice. Meanwhile, smaller icebreakers keep Arctic rivers, harbors, and channels ice-free in winter. A few specially equipped icebreakers act as expedition ships for scientific investigations in the Arctic and Antarctic.

Large or small, icebreakers are built to a common plan. Usually the bows are strengthened, reinforced internally, and undercut or spoon-shaped. The strengthening (often with stainless steel) allows them to meet ice head-on without damage; the undercutting allows them

An icebreaker rises onto the ice in order to cut a way through.

to charge the ice, rise slightly onto it, and break it down with their weight. Some produce curtains of bubbles along the bow, to help in dispersing the ice they have cut. Propellers are often protected by tunnels or cages, which keep them from being chipped or broken by lumps of ice. There are usually several engines capable of being linked to at least two main propellers; often there are "bow thrusters"—small propellers mounted sideways near the bow—that help in turning and maneuvering. The propellers slip readily into reverse, so the icebreaker can back without difficulty down a channel that it has cut.

Icebreakers use their weight and momentum to shift ice. If trapped and unable to move in newly formed ice, they are almost helpless. To avoid this hazard, many have internal tanks with powerful pumps that allow them to shift fuel rapidly from side to side or from bow to stern. Thus they can roll and pitch, creating the small space around them necessary for movement. In

unfamiliar waters or for especially difficult tasks they often work in pairs, so they can come to each other's aid.

Most icebreakers are diesel-driven, but some of the largest are nuclear-powered, allowing them to stay long periods at sea without refueling. The most powerful are able to cut through sheets of solid ice over 6 feet thick at steady speeds of 8 to 10 knots and batter their way through even heavier ice by repeated ramming. However, this is not what they most often do. Cutting and battering are expensive in fuel, and impose heavy wear on ships and crews alike.

More important in everyday running is the ability of these ships to manipulate ice—to maneuver in leads and small spaces, push floes and icebergs out of the way, and open channels between floes for other ships to use. To do all this safely, and to be able to escape should the ice close on them, they need skilled, experienced operators, who run them economically and hold the vessels' special strengths in reserve for emergency use.

Arctic sea ice is heavier and more persistent in some years than in others. In 1983 more than 50 cargo ships were trapped in the ice off northeastern Siberia: It took every available icebreaker to free them by the end of the season. In 1990, a much easier year for ice, the nuclear icebreaker *Rossiya* made the first-ever tourist cruise to the North Pole. Leaving Murmansk on July 31, she pushed through some of the heaviest Arctic ice to reach the North Pole on August 8, and returned to Murmansk just over one week later.

Trapped in the pack ice

Problems with pack ice have altered the course of many polar expeditions, none more so than the Canadian Arctic Expedition of 1913–1918.

Karluk, the expedition ship, was a Canadian vessel of about 250 tons, stoutly built of timber, with sails and a small steam engine—well used to working in ice. The expedition intended to work along the northern Canadian coast, but became trapped in pack ice off northern Alaska in October 1913. The ice was drifting westward and for three wintery months the little ship had to drift westward with it, held safely but firmly, and quite unable to escape.

Early January found the ship north of Wrangell Island, off the Siberian coast. There the tightly packed floes came under heavy pressure, groaning, creaking, and rising into ridges that surrounded and dwarfed the ship. Suddenly *Karluk* was forced upward and over to one side. Fearing the worst, passengers and crew unloaded as much of their expedition equipment as they could, setting up camp on the ice. The party was made up of 22 men, one woman, two children, 16 dogs, and a cat. After several days of intermittent pressure, ice eventually forced its way through *Karluk*'s thick planking, and the sea poured in.

It was close to midwinter, bitterly cold, and dark for most of each day. However, the expedition had two wooden huts, sledges, boats, and plenty of food and spare clothing. Among the members were a family of Inuit, who knew well how to survive in the Arctic.

The *Endurance*, caught in pack ice in the Antarctic.

Within a few days groups were sent off with dog teams toward Wrangell Island, dimly visible 75 miles to the south. After many mishaps on the treacherous sea ice, all but four people arrived there safely, camping on a low sandy spit on the north side. In mid-March the captain set out with one Inuit companion to sled to the Siberian mainland for help. It was an all but impossible journey for dogs and men, across steep pressure ridges and wide leads, but they succeeded. On September 8 the *Karluk* survivors—including the ship's cat—were finally rescued.

In the following year in the Antarctic, Ernest Shackleton's ship *Endurance* became caught on ice. Even with an auxiliary steam engine, the ship was not powerful enough to force her way out. For over nine months she drifted helplessly more than 1,500 miles until, in early November, great pressure ridges developed within the ice. *Endurance* resisted stoutly, but eventually began to break up. She sank on November 21, leaving 28 men and over 60 sled dogs in a tented camp on the ice. Shackleton wrote:

The remains of the stone hut built by the stranded crew of a Swedish ship.

"The attack of the ice reached its climax at 4 P.M. The ship was hove stern up by the pressure, and the drifting floe, moving laterally across the stern, split the rudder and tore out the rudder-post and stern-post. Then, while we watched, the ice loosened and the *Endurance* sank a little. The decks were breaking upwards and the water was pouring in below. [One hour later] It was a sickening sensation to feel the decks breaking up under one's feet, the great beams bending and then snapping with a noise like heavy gun-fire. . . . The floes were simply annihilating the ship."

Ten years before this, a Swedish ship had gotten stuck in the pack ice in the Weddell Sea (see map on page 10), less than 20 miles from land. The 22 men on board walked ashore across the ice, and built a stone hut in which to spend the bitter winter. They lived off the ship's supplies, and seals and penguins, and all but one survived until the following summer when another ship rescued them.

Tragedy of the *Titanic*

The most famous ship to be lost to ice was the passenger liner *Titanic*, completed in 1912 and the largest ship afloat. Equipped with every possible safety device, she was even claimed to be unsinkable. However, in the early morning of April 15, 1912, on her maiden voyage across the North Atlantic Ocean, the *Titanic* ran at full speed into an iceberg. This was not sea ice, but ice that had originated on land, probably in a glacier along the Greenland coast.

This berg was large enough to slit a long gash in the ship's bow, and the *Titanic* immediately began to sink. Though the sea was calm and visibility good, 1,513 passengers and crew were lost from a total of 2,224 people on board. The *Titanic* has since been discovered and photographed on the ocean bed.

Today, aircraft and satellite images report ice movements, and nearly all ships are equipped with radar, which shows the presence of pack ice and icebergs.

CHAPTER FIVE

SNOW ON THE MOVE

Snowfall

Soft snow recently fallen is made up of thin, transparent ice crystals with delicate feathery edges. Their shapes can be seen through a magnifying glass. Usually they are six-sided, bluish crystals with beautiful sculptured patterns. Breathe on them, and you will see how quickly they disappear, feather edges first, then the crystal bodies. Hoarfrost, rime, hailstones, and the feathery patterns that grow on windows in winter are other forms of ice crystals.

In Britain and other warm temperate lands close to sea level a snowfall seldom lasts more than a few hours, leaving up to three feet of soft snow. Winds and thaw soon pack this down to a thin layer. In the cold forests of Finland and northern Canada a single snowfall may last for several days, leaving up to ten feet of soft snow. Successive falls can bring the level of snow up to the eaves of houses, keeping everyone busy digging out doorways and clearing roads. Snow that falls in October and November can still be around in March and April. When the spring thaw melts it, the resulting water pours away in floods, filling lakes and swelling streams to torrential rivers.

In the mountains

Countries such as Switzerland, and the alpine regions of Italy and Austria, have peaks that rise high above the snow line, the limit of permanent snow. This means that the peaks have year-round ice and snow, and often glaciers that form high up and cascade down to lower levels.

Alpine regions have high grassy meadows that are clear of snow in summer. These are often damp enough to grow long, lush grass, where farmers graze cattle and sheep. In late autumn the animals are brought down to lower ground, often to be kept indoors through the winter.

Meanwhile, heavy snow builds up on the high grasslands. When the snow is thick and reliable, the Alps become winter resorts for skiing, supporting a huge tourist industry that brings prosperity to the upland areas.

There are similar alpine regions in southeast Australia (the Snowy Mountains of Victoria, for example), in New Zealand's South Island, and throughout the western mountains of the United States. So popular has skiing become as a winter sport that all these areas now gain far more from tourism than from farming.

In the European Alps sheep are moved down the mountain in autumn to spend the winter in the lowlands.

History frozen

In polar regions where there are permanent ice caps, snowfall is not necessarily heavier than in temperate regions. However, because of the cold, much of the snow fails to melt in summer; instead it builds up year after year. In southern Greenland and along parts of the coast of Antarctica, snowfall is particularly heavy. In northern Greenland and on the high plateau of Antarctica, annual snowfall is much lighter but the colder conditions still produce long-lasting ice sheets, growing to a mile or more thick and lasting for years without melting.

Samples of ice drilled from the depths of the world's thickest ice caps have been found to be many thousands of years old. Scientists have discovered how to tell their age and gather from them all kinds of hidden information about climates and living conditions of long ago.

Within the ice are bubbles of air, and tiny particles of rock dust, volcanic ash, and pollutants that were present in the atmosphere at the time the snow was falling. A core of ice only 4 inches in diameter, drilled from an ice sheet, contains a valuable record of events and conditions long ago. From the Antarctic ice sheet, which in places reaches up to 3 miles thick, several cores more than 1,600 feet deep have been drilled, some more than 6,500 feet. From the longest cores, the bottom ice is probably hundreds of thousands of years old.

Careful examination and analysis of the cores shows the presence in them of layers of ash, some of which can be traced to known volcanic eruptions. These act as age markers. Chemical analysis of ice laid down over the last few decades shows increasing levels of pollutants; for example, lead has increased, due to its increasing use in gasoline. Radioactivity from nuclear tests appears in the recent record. From

Trees in Norway half buried by winter snowfalls.

much older ice the decay of radioactive materials can be used to put date tags at different depths, and the ratios of two kinds of oxygen can reveal the temperature that prevailed when the snow was falling, giving us a record of changing temperatures over many years.

Disappearing huts

In parts of Antarctica and on the Greenland ice cap, where the snow never melts, a single-story expedition house built on the surface will be halfway up to the eaves in snow within a year, and almost completely covered in two to three years. Within four or five years it will have disappeared altogether. This means that it can be reached only down long staircases and through tunnels. After a few more years an ordinary hut becomes useless, for the weight of snow crushes it and makes it unsafe to live in.

To tackle this problem, engineers have designed expedition huts that are built inside huge corrugated steel tubes, which can take the weight of the overlying snow. The huts are reached down long staircases, which have to be extended in length every year to reach the surface. Chimneys and ventilators, too, have to be extended to reach the surface. Supplies are taken down to the huts along sloping tunnels. An alternative is to build the huts on platforms that can be raised every year. Each summer hydraulic jacks are used to lift the huts above the new surface, ready for next winter's storms.

These tubes protect the living quarters of a research station in the Antarctic.

Hailstorms

Hail is a kind of frozen rain that falls from towering storm clouds. Inside these clouds there are strong updrafts, which whirl the raindrops up and around. In the cold air the raindrops freeze, and the frozen pellets gather more water to them, forming frozen layers on the outside. The longer the hailstones stay in the cloud, the bigger they grow before falling. Hailstones as big as peas are not unusual. When they fall they can sting, and a hailstorm with stones this size in spring can do a lot of damage to gardens and crops.

Occasionally hailstones can be much bigger—the size of marbles or even small eggs. Storms with hailstones that size often occur in temperate and tropical countries, where heat from the ground causes big, towering clouds that give the stones plenty of chance to grow. Marble-size hailstones can bring severe damage, stripping trees of their leaves, breaking windows and roof shingles, even killing people and animals.

Blizzards and drifts

Strong winds immediately after a snowfall whip the snow back into the air and whirl it around. A blizzard of wind and snow can be dangerous to travel in. Blown snow blocks the windshields of cars and aircraft, making it hard for anyone to see out, especially at night. The wind gathers the snow together in drifts many feet thick, hard-packed and difficult to shift. Even a light fall of snow can be blown into drifts thick enough to block roads, runways, and railroad lines. Climbers and walkers caught out in blizzards find them exhausting and chilling, and can easily lose their sense of direction.

In polar regions particular snow conditions can be critical for human safety. Lightly blown snow packs down smoothly to create an even surface; hard-blown snow develops ridges and furrows called sastrugi, difficult to walk on and even more difficult to pull a sledge through (see pages 13 and 19).

Avalanches on this mountainside in Canada have repeatedly cleared all the trees in their path, leaving evidence of the direction they usually take. (Inset) An avalanche on Mt. McKinley, Alaska.

Avalanche conditions

On level ground snow usually stays in place until it melts and disappears. On hillsides it is less stable. When enough has gathered it can shift, sliding downward into the valleys in avalanches. Damaging avalanches can occur in hilly country after any heavy snowfall, when the newly settled snow begins to flow downhill. But really big avalanches usually involve snow that has been gathering and lying around for some weeks or months. These are the dangerous avalanches—the kind that sweep away trees, houses, and even villages, and sometimes kill many people. In the summer of 1962 disaster struck a beautiful valley of the South American Andes Mountains. From the summit of Mt. Huascaran, 20,700 feet above sea level, some 180,000 cubic feet of snow and ice suddenly cascaded down into the valley, bringing with them thousands of tons of rock. This huge destructive mass fell more than 13,000 feet, moving at a speed that observers estimated to be about 37 mph, overwhelming 10 miles of fertile land dotted with farms and settlements. Before grinding to a standstill it had destroyed nine small towns, killing more than 400 people and many hundreds of farm animals.

The snow and ice that gathers on a mountainside in autumn and winter is at first usually dry enough to stay in place. It builds up a little with each new snowfall, but is too light and well packed together to move downhill. As time goes on, the structure of the snow crystals changes. Those nearest the ground, instead of interlocking, become slippery and begin to slide over each other. So even in winter the snow on a hillside may start to move, and slide down into the valley below.

"Dry avalanches," as these are called, are not usually extensive or dangerous, unless snowfall has been sudden and very heavy. Often dry avalanches start accidentally, but sometimes they can be started intentionally. Where they are likely to be damaging, it pays to take control of them, and make them happen before they get too big. In ski resorts and mountain villages where dry avalanches could be dangerous,

Wooden or steel barriers can help to hold back the snow and prevent avalanches. These are in Switzerland.

rangers go up the mountains and start small slides, usually with explosive charges, to prevent bigger ones from happening later.

Much more damaging are "wet avalanches," which usually happen in late winter or spring when the snow has started to melt. As the air warms in the spring, surface layers of snow thaw, and the resulting water trickles down into the lower layers, filling spaces between the crystals. After a time so much water gathers that the saturated snow below the surface can no longer support its own weight. Then it starts to slide downhill, gathering speed and taking more snow into itself as it goes. Soon all the snow on the hillside—perhaps tens of thousands of tons of wet, soggy snow—is on the move, and there is very little that can withstand its rush.

At some point when the snow becomes unstable, any slight movement can start an avalanche. A small earth tremor may do so, or an aircraft flying by, a gunshot, a car backfiring; even a shout may be enough to start the movement. Even the weight of a skier may be enough to start an avalanche rolling.

Safety on the ski slopes

As more people learn to ski, and new sports such as snow surfing and paragliding have been developed, more and more winter sports participants are drawn away from the marked ski trails to the untouched slopes of deep snow. But the danger of avalanches often lurks there. The Swiss Institute for Snow and Avalanche Research points out that one hour after an avalanche accident, only three or four victims of every ten completely covered by snow can be rescued alive. It is vital, therefore, that winter sports enthusiasts take the danger of avalanches seriously.

Avalanche danger increases with the increasing angle of the slope, but avalanches can occur even on slopes of an angle as low as 30°. Slopes in the shade are more likely to be dangerous than sunny slopes. The avalanche danger increases in direct proportion to the quantity of newly fallen snow. The most critical period, therefore, is the first fine day after a period of bad weather. The avalanche danger is greatest when wind follows a snowfall.

In ski resorts, people with little or no knowledge of avalanches should keep to marked ski trails. Signs and barriers warn of dangerous conditions, and avalanche bulletins are given on the radio and television, and in the newspapers.

The advice to anyone who witnesses an avalanche accident is first to observe exactly the stages of the accident. Next, mark the entry tracks and vanishing points of those buried, for example with ski poles. Begin searching immediately, with electronic searching equipment if available. Search with eyes and ears the avalanche area below the vanishing points of those buried. Dig out any equipment which is discovered, but let it lie on the snow where it was found.

If a buried person is found, then free the head, give first aid and warmth. Let the accident victim remain in the snow hole until outside assistance arrives, and raise the alarm.

Survivors say that to be caught up in an avalanche is like being tumbled in a heavy sea.

The first impact throws you over and knocks the breath out of you, making it difficult to run or shout warnings. Rolling over and over within the snow, you lose all sense of direction. The pressure of snow may pin you down, preventing movement and restricting your breathing. If the snow is wet and heavy, bones may be broken.

People who live in avalanche country are always prepared for the worst, with skilled community rescue services on call. When an avalanche has occurred that is known to involve human casualties, first on the scene are usually groups of dog handlers with trained dogs—German shepherds, collies, or Labradors. These are highly efficient in scenting victims under the snow. Groups of volunteers form lines to probe the snow with long thin rods, while medical teams stand by with tents, blankets, and warmth. In the past, rescue parties might take several hours to reach the victims, slogging through the snow with stretchers or light sleds. Now, they are more likely to take minutes by helicopter or ski-equipped aircraft.

Skiers need to be aware of the danger of avalanches.

CHAPTER SIX

OUT IN THE COLD

Where does cold come from?

For both Eurasia and North America the north is always colder than the south. In middle latitudes north winds bring cold from the Arctic, and south winds bring warmth from the tropics. Cold and warm air meet along a boundary called the polar front. The polar front wriggles and shifts as weather systems move along it. Those who live well north of it experience Arctic conditions most of the time, and those who live well to the south are usually warm. But

The thin layer of ice and snow in this winter scene could quickly thaw.

those who live near the front—and that includes many millions of Americans and Europeans of middle latitudes—must expect alternating spells of warm and cold in their daily weather.

All year round, but especially in winter, the northeastern Atlantic Ocean is kept remarkably warm by the North Atlantic Drift. This is a strong marine current that flows from the Caribbean Sea (where it is called the Gulf Stream) across to northern Norway and beyond. In the depths of winter, when almost everywhere north of the Arctic Circle is frozen up, this warm water from the southwest ensures that the northeastern Atlantic stays ice-free.

Western Europe stands at a crossroads of weather; hence its extremely variable climate. In summer, cool northerly winds alternate with warm southerlies, often in cycles as successive depressions sweep over from west to east. In winter the effects are intensified. Cold moist maritime air from Greenland and the northwest, at near-freezing temperatures, brings snow flurries to Britain and maritime Europe. Even colder east winds blow in from central Europe and the Commonwealth of Independent States, bringing bitter weather with subzero temperatures. Yet within a few hours these can be replaced by damp southwesterly air, warmed over the North Atlantic Drift, bringing spells of mild, rainy weather.

Adapting to cold

Humans are designed for living in temperate or tropical climates and do not adapt well to polar climates, or even to winter cold. Among the least furry of all mammals, we have little built-in protection. For thousands of years we have had to rely on fire and the skins and wool of other animals to keep us warm. Today we use central heating to keep the air around us warm, eat plenty of food to maintain our own heat output,

These workers, in modern suits, are surveying the structure of glacier ice as part of oil exploration in Svalbard.

and wear a range of fabrics that help to keep our body heat in. We need particularly good insulation if we venture into cold regions. People who leave temperate regions to work in cold climates acclimatize only slightly. After a few days or weeks their skin becomes a little less sensitive to cold. Some of the early explorers speeded the process by having cold showers or rubbing themselves with snow. Modern workers in cold climates spend much of their time in warmth, exposing themselves as little as possible to the discomforts and dangers of cold. Huts, tents, drilling rigs, ships, aircraft, and houses are all well heated.

Those whose work takes them outside no longer wear animal skins and furs—they are too heavy and bulky, especially for active people. The trend today is to wear light fabrics in several layers, usually starting with cellular underwear that traps air close to the skin. Over that come loosely woven shirts and trousers, ventilated to allow air to circulate and carry away sweat. Outside come padded suits, filled with down, wool, or synthetic flock, and covered with tightly woven cotton or nylon to keep the wind out. A hood lined with synthetic fur, two or three pairs of socks, fabric or nylon boots, and several pairs of gloves or mitts complete the outfit. Sometimes the hoods are edged with real animal fur, which sheds ice more readily than synthetics. Too much clothing is likely to cause sweating and discomfort; it may even be dangerous, for the sweat creates internal damp and robs you of valuable heat.

The native Inuit of the Arctic are physically

How cold is cold?

32°F	The freezing point of fresh water and a little above the freezing point of sea water; about the mean summer temperature at the North Pole, and for some of the warmer Antarctic islands.
14°F	A cold winter day in New York City; cool for a summer day in coastal Antarctica.
−4°F	Seldom experienced in Britain and rare in lowland Europe; not unusual in alpine regions in winter, and a mean winter temperature for some coastal Antarctic stations.
−22°F	The mean winter temperature of the Arctic basin: not at all uncommon in the streets of some Canadian Arctic towns in January and February, and close to the mean summer temperature at the South Pole.
−40°F	A cold winter's day on the coast of Antarctica, and in the colder regions of Siberia and Canada; almost cold enough for mercury thermometers to freeze.
−58°F	A cold winter's temperature for coastal Antarctica; rare anywhere else except on the Antarctica plateau and the coldest parts of Canada and Siberia. Uncomfortable to work outdoors.
−76°F	Close to the winter mean for the South Pole; a very cold day in Siberia, and too cold for most people to stay outside for long.
−129.28°F	Lowest temperature recorded on earth, at Vostok, on the high Antarctic plateau.

To convert a temperature in °F to its equivalent in °C, first subtract 32, then divide by 1.8. To convert a temperature in °C to its equivalent in °F, multiply by 1.8 and add 32.

European workers in the polar regions suffer from the cold, even with plenty of special clothing.

Australian aborigines can cope with extremes of hot and cold, with little or no clothing.

not much better adapted to deal with cold than are Europeans; their success lies more in how they live. They are short, squat people—a shape that may help them to retain body heat better than tall, thin people. Their diet often contains more fat than Americans would tolerate, useful in keeping them warm. But through folklore and everyday practice they know more about avoiding cold and danger than most nonnatives. They know when to work and when to stay indoors, how to dress for different kinds of activity, and where to find new kinds of food if old ones run out. They expect cold. They are not upset or frightened by it, but are happy to avoid it whenever they can.

Far better adapted to cold are Australian aborigines and African bushmen. Since they live in some of the world's hottest climates, they spend much of their time naked and outdoors. Exposed to extreme heat during the day, they often experience cold—almost to the freezing point—at night. Aborigines and bushmen seem to be much less affected by cold than Americans. A bushman can sleep comfortably with very little covering through the night, while his American companion lies awake, shivering miserably and waiting for the dawn.

The Fuegian Indians of Tierra del Fuego in southern South America lived almost naked in a very cold environment. They sometimes wore skins, but not usually when hunting. Early European visitors to their shores were astonished to find Fuegians swimming in near-freezing water and hunting semi-naked in snowstorms. The naturalist Charles Darwin met them on Woollaston Island, off Tierra del Fuego, in February 1834, and was horrified to find humans living in such squalid conditions. This is how he described their primitive housing:

"Any little depression in the soil is chosen, over this a few rotten trunks of trees are placed, and to windward some tufts of grass. Here five or six human beings, naked and uncovered from the wind, rain and snow in this tempestuous climate, sleep on the wet ground, coiled up like animals."

Food was little better than housing:

"In the morning, they rise to pick shell fish at low water, and the women, winter and summer, dive to collect sea eggs [small fish]; such miserable food is eked out by tasteless berries and fungi."

Darwin wondered what could have tempted tribes from tropical and warm temperate regions to migrate south and live in so dreadful a place. In fact the Fuegians died out soon afterward, not from cold, but probably from diseases introduced by early European visitors and settlers.

Cold deserts

Though we usually think of deserts as hot dry places, they can be *cold* and dry, too. Deserts occur wherever there is little or no precipitation—rain or snow—throughout the year.

There is an extensive desert in north Greenland, for example; while southern Greenland receives heavy snow all year round, enough to maintain a thick ice cap, northern Greenland is much farther from the warm, moist North Atlantic winds and receives virtually no snow or rain.

There are similar desert areas in Antarctica, kept free of ice by lack of winds off the sea. Rather confusingly they are called "oases"—though an oasis is usually a green area within a desert. Antarctic oases are ice-free and, because they are so dry, they have very little vegetation, either—just bare rock and gravel where hardly anything grows.

Temperate regions also have cold desert areas. The Gobi Desert, in Mongolia, is one of the largest deserts in the world. Here summers are often hot and dry, the heat tempered only by the desert's being so high above sea level. Winters are bitterly cold, down to −22°F or lower, again with very little snow or rain.

Bactrian camels in the Gobi Desert.

Frostbite

When fingers, faces, and toes are exposed to extreme cold, the arteries and veins in them constrict, and no blood flows to them. After a few minutes they turn numb, becoming white and waxy-looking. These are the danger signs of frostbite. Often you cannot tell that your cheek or ear has become affected; companions keep an eye on each other, and warn when they see the signs.

The immediate action is to warm the affected part: If this can be done quickly, by gentle rubbing or the application of a warm hand, there is no lasting damage. But if the chilling continues, the skin and underlying tissues that are starved of blood may freeze.

Many polar explorers and mountaineers have suffered permanent damage—skin scarring and loss of fingers or toes, for example—through neglected frostbite. The American explorer Robert Peary, in a journey toward the North Pole in 1899, noted after a particularly tough march across sea ice that his right foot felt "wooden." In the warmth of the camp that night his companions cut off his sealskin boots, to find that both legs were frostbitten and bloodless up to the knees. When they took off his inner socks, several toes fell away with them. "There is no time to pamper sick men on the trail," snapped Peary, adding that "a few toes were not much to give to achieve the Pole."

When European medical scientists became interested in frostbite, they began by studying

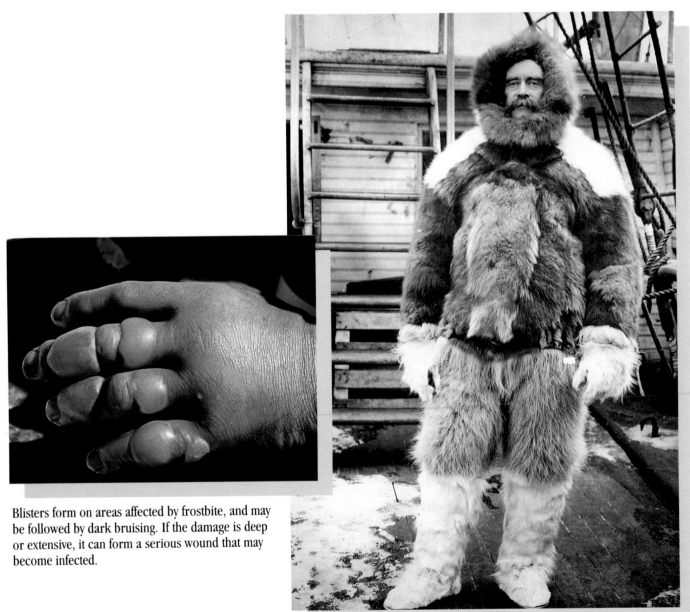

Blisters form on areas affected by frostbite, and may be followed by dark bruising. If the damage is deep or extensive, it can form a serious wound that may become infected.

Robert Peary lost several toes from frostbite.

Some Lapps in Norway and Finland still follow the traditional life-style of reindeer herding. They use old skills to deal with the cold—this herder is insulating his boots with a special grass.

the Inuit of northern Canada and Alaska, whom they thought would know all about it. But they found to their surprise that these native people hardly ever get frostbitten—every young Inuit learns how to avoid it. The worst sufferers in the north (apart from explorers) were European settlers who were careless enough to get caught out in the cold, and did not know how to cope.

Hypothermia

When we feel cold, it is usually because our skin temperature has fallen a little, though body temperature as a whole may still be close to the normal 98.6°F (37°C). Our first defense is to become more alert and active, and to shiver. This is a muscle shake which, like any other muscular activity, generates internal heat. Walking, running, and jumping also get us warm quickly. Old people and invalids can shiver, but may not be able to keep active; hence their need to be in warm rooms and out of drafts.

If chilling continues, the body's internal temperature starts to fall. At a body temperature of 88°F to 89.6°F shivering can become quite violent, so that ordinary work and thinking are impossible. Shivering, like exercise, uses up a lot of energy. Even young and healthy people, if they are thinly clothed, wet, or in a cold wind, soon become tired, and may not be able to continue at so high an energy output. They begin to feel lazy, sluggish, and ready to sleep. It is important at this stage to get them into shelter out of the wind. A cave or trench in the snow can help; so does a stove or a fire, even a small one.

On further chilling even shivering stops, because blood is no longer circulating efficiently and the muscles are starved of fuel. At body temperatures 40°F to 50°F below normal, nerves and muscles no longer work together. The

Emperor penguins (here, adults and young) are insulated against the Antarctic cold.

victim now cannot think clearly, and becomes clumsy and is liable to fall. A very cold person loses all sense of danger and just wants to lie down and sleep. Two or three degrees lower still, and we lose consciousness, and the heartbeat becomes irregular and eventually stops. When people die of hypothermia, or abnormally low body temperature, this is usually what has happened.

Several people together can huddle, reducing the overall surface to keep in as much body heat as they can. This is how emperor penguins manage to incubate their eggs in the depths of the Antarctic winter. By huddling with hundreds of others, each emperor loses only 20 percent as much heat as he would if he were standing alone.

People who have become very cold need time to warm up. William Scoresby, a whaling captain who sailed many seasons off Greenland during the early 19th century, was one of the first to recognize the effects of severe chilling. When a dozen of his crew were recovered after being lost for over 12 hours in open boats, he stopped their shipmates from taking them below decks immediately to warm up by the stove. Instead, the mens' hands, feet, and faces were rubbed to restore circulation, and "those who were capable of the exertion were made to run about the deck, chasing or being chased, one by the other . . . until some glow of warmth, and consciousness of restored circulation, had taken place of the pre-existing chilliness or insensibility." Only then were they allowed below, and all survived without permanent injury.

A cold swim

Cold water draws heat from your body even faster than cold winds. In temperate seas at 60°F we can survive for several hours; in seas close to the freezing point we may be lucky to survive longer than a few minutes. If you fall into cold water fully clothed, keep at least some of your clothes on. They will not keep you warm, but by holding a layer of warmth next to your skin they slow down the rate of cooling, and may help you to survive longer.

What to do next depends very much on where you are. If you are close to land or safety, swim toward it and get out of the water as fast as you can. If you cannot swim or are unable to swim far enough, and help is likely, stay where you are. Swimming uses up energy and makes you lose heat quickly. You will probably survive better by staying fairly still, holding on to anything that will keep you afloat. That way you will keep conscious longer—perhaps long enough for help to reach you.

Animal insulation

Cold-blooded animals—fish, reptiles, and insects, for example—do not need insulating. Their bodies run at the temperature of their environment, whatever it may be. Warm-

Reindeer are insulated with fur and a layer of blubber, which they draw on when food is scarce toward the end of winter.

blooded animals—birds and mammals—have to maintain a high and constant body temperature, usually 96.8°F to 98.6°F, whatever the temperature outside them. They do this by "burning" or breaking down high-energy fuels that they have taken in as food, mostly carbohydrates (starchy foods and sugar) and fats, then using their insulation to keep in the heat they have generated. All birds and nearly all mammals are well insulated with feathers or fur, and many have an extra layer of insulation—fat or "blubber"—under the skin.

Fur, feathers, and clothing all insulate in the same way—by trapping a layer of warm air against the body, and keeping cold air out. Among birds, emperor penguins are perhaps the best insulated, with curved feathers that overlap like tiles on a roof, each feather with a tuft of down at the base. The feathers form a thick outer layer, waterproof as well as wind-tight; the down forms an undershirt that traps the air inside. The harder the wind blows, the more tightly the feathers pack together. Among mammals, reindeer have some of the best-insulating

fur. Each hair is hollow and air-filled, and the fur is so tightly packed that the strongest gales cannot penetrate.

Blubber is a layer of fat stored under the skin. The animal uses it as an emergency store for when food is scarce, but it is also good insulation. Blood vessels pass through it to supply the skin. When the animal is cold, these surface vessels constrict, so both the skin and the blubber cool, and less heat is lost from the body. Whales and seals, especially, use blubber for insulation: in the biggest whales, over 98 ft. long, the blubber may be almost 20 inches thick. Whales have often been hunted, for the blubber yields oil that can be burned as fuel, or turned into foods such as margarine for people.

Reindeer and penguins, too, have blubber under their skin, just an inch or so thick. In bad weather both penguins and reindeer turn to face the wind, exposing as little of their surface as possible to it. So efficient is their insulation that snow settles on them without melting. Whereas sheep trap snow and ice in their fleeces, and in bad weather often die of exposure, reindeer shake off the snow and remain dry. Sometimes they allow a mask of ice to build up on their faces, which seems not to bother them and may help to keep the wind out.

As we have seen in this book, humans are far less well adapted to cold than most mammals. Although people living and working in cold regions have developed many practical ways of dealing with snow, ice, and cold, it is perhaps their respect for the harsh climate that provides a key to preventing unnecessary damage by bad weather. While we cannot prevent the arrival of snow and ice, or the lowering of air temperatures, we can limit their effects not only by being well prepared but also by avoiding any unnecessary risks.

GLOSSARY

fjord—a long, narrow inlet of sea between steep cliffs. Fjords are common on the coast of Norway.

floe (ice floe)—a sheet of ice floating on the sea.

frostbite—the destruction of skin tissue caused by exposure to intense cold.

fast ice—ice on the sea that is fixed to the edge of the land.

glacier—a mass of ice formed on land where snow is packed down by wind and its own weight until it forms clear ice. Glaciers appear to be still, but they do move very slowly.

hypothermia—lowering of the body temperature. Elderly people suffer from hypothermia in very cold weather, and sometimes die from it.

iceberg—a mass of floating ice that has broken away from a glacier.

ice cap—a mass of ice and snow that permanently covers an area of land or a mountain peak.

latitude—the distance measured in degrees north or south of the equator. (Polar latitudes, temperate latitudes or regions.)

mean (summer/winter) temperature—average temperature over a period of time.

pack ice—a mass of ice floating on the sea, usually made up of floes broken from bigger sheets.

pemmican—a paste of shredded dried meat, fat, and cereal, often provided in emergency rations.

permafrost—ground that is permanently frozen, although the top layer may thaw briefly in summer.

snowfield—a large area of permanent snow.

snow line—the line on a high mountain that marks the limit of permanent snow.

tundra—a kind of patchy, low-lying vegetation; also the vast area in the Arctic where this vegetation is found.

whiteout—a loss of visibility and sense of direction caused by thick white cloud and white snow cover.

INDEX